COULD A SHARK DO GYMNASTICS?

...and other questions

Aleksei Bitskoff &
Camilla de la Bédoyère

QED Publishing

A great white shark

Design: Duck Egg Blue
Editors: Ruth Symons and Carly Madden
Editorial Director: Victoria Garrard
Art Director: Laura Roberts-Jensen

Copyright © QED Publishing 2015

First published in the UK in 2015 by
QED Publishing
A Quarto Group company
The Old Brewery
6 Blundell Street
London N7 9BH

www.qed-publishing.co.uk

A catalogue record for this book is available from the British Library.

ISBN 978 1 78171 581 9

Printed in China

is a **huge,** meat-eating fish.

He swims through the world's oceans, hunting other animals to eat.

Imagine a great white shark came to stay. What do you think would happen?

What if a shark went to a waterpark?

It would be his idea of a **great day out!**

Sharks are just the right shape for speeding through water – or zooooming down slides!

He'd like the pools best. Sharks are fish, so they have gills for breathing underwater.

He would be there a long time. Great white sharks have nearly **240 teeth!**

He wouldn't need a filling. Sharks lose teeth all the time but they keep **growing** new ones.

How would a shark get to school?

He is far too **big** to squeeze inside a car, so you could strap him to the roof!

Great white sharks can grow up to **6 metres long**, but most are about 4.5 metres. That's the length of a family car!

Even a newborn great white shark is **bigger than you!**

What if a shark had a party?

He would have a barbecue because sharks loooooooove to eat meat!

In the sea, great white sharks eat seals and fish. But at a barbecue, he would eat about 5000 sausages in one go.

He wouldn't need to eat again for two weeks!

Could a shark do gymnastics?

Sharks have **strong** and **bendy bodies** that are perfect for gymnastics.

He could **leap high** over a bar. Great white sharks jump right out of the water to catch seals, sea lions and seabirds.

Their awesome leaps can reach more than **2.5 metres.**

That's higher than any human has ever jumped!

Could a shark play tennis?

A shark would be great at ball games.
He could use his big fins or powerful tail to hit a ball.

A shark would always know where the ball is because he has **super senses.**

2 5 30
0 0 0

Sharks know when fish are swimming **behind** or **below** them, and can even sense their heartbeats!

What if a shark needed the loo?

He could find the loos with his eyes shut just by following his nose.

When a shark smells wee in the ocean, it means there's a yummy sea creature nearby.

Sharks have an amazing sense of smell. They could smell a teaspoon of wee in a whole swimming pool!

Could a shark play on a seesaw?

He would need a **big** seesaw, and **lots of children** to help balance him.

A fully grown great white shark weighs about 2000 kilograms.

That's the same weight
as a rhinoceros or nearly
100 children!

Would a shark like to play in the snow?

He would **love it!**

Great white sharks don't mind getting chilly because they live in cool oceans.

Whooshing downhill on a sledge would be just as much fun as speeding through the sea.

Fast sharks can swim almost **ten times faster** than a human!

More about great white sharks

Great white shark is pointing to the places where he lives. Can you see where you live?

FACT FILE

Sharks are a type of fish that live in the ocean. They have rough skin and sharp teeth.

There are more than 400 different types of shark.

Sharks have been around for 350 million years. That means there were sharks before there were dinosaurs!

The largest sharks in the world are called whale sharks. They grow to 12 metres long. That's as big as a bus.

Although sharks look scary, very few are dangerous to humans. Most sharks are shy and prefer to stay away from us!

Areas where great white sharks live

NORTH AMERICA

PACIFIC OCEAN

SOUT
AMERI

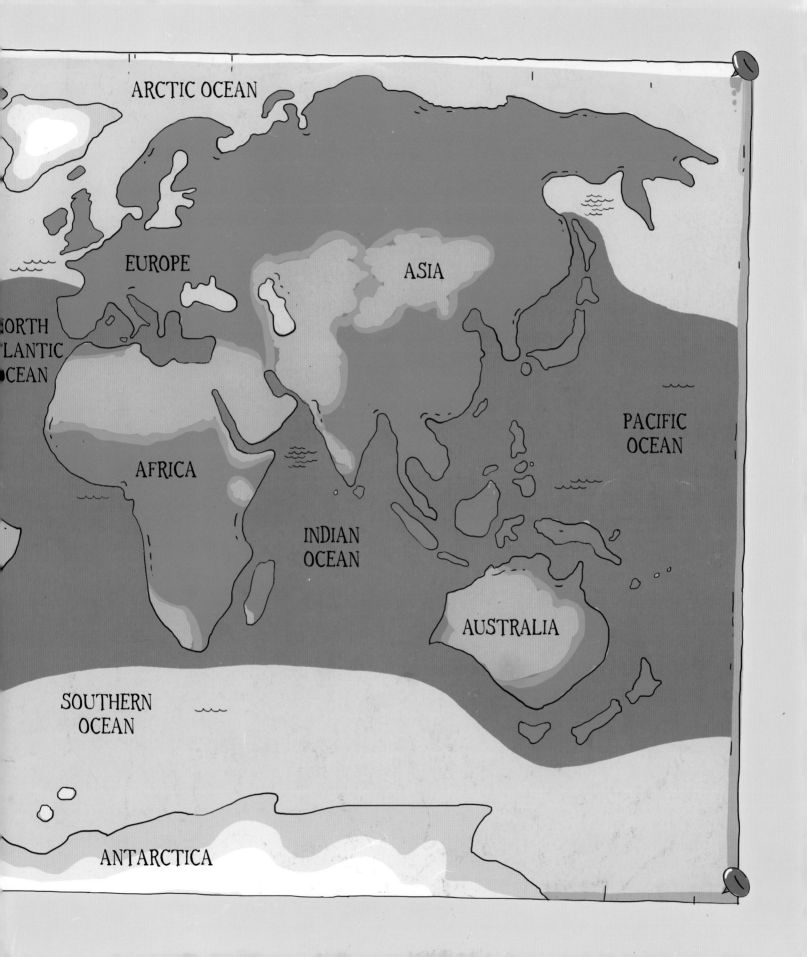

Greetings from Florida!

POST CARD

It's great to be back in my ocean home. I was really missing the deep cold water. As soon as I arrived all the seals and fish disappeared from view – I can't imagine why! Anyway, I'm feeling a bit peckish so I'd better go. Catch up with you again some time.
Love,
Great White Shark X

The Jensen Family
167 Dugdale Road
Hertfordshire
CB21 4ZA
UK

1348263560205278762